W9-BIS-606

M

Zero Is
Not Nothing

Zero Is Not Nothing

by Mindel and Harry Sitomer

illustrated by Richard Cuffari

Thomas Y. Crowell   New York

YOUNG MATH BOOKS

Edited by Dr. Max Beberman, Director of the Committee on School Mathematics Projects, University of Illinois

BIGGER AND SMALLER

CIRCLES

COMPUTERS

THE ELLIPSE

ESTIMATION

FRACTIONS ARE PARTS OF THINGS

GRAPH GAMES

LINES, SEGMENTS, POLYGONS

LONG, SHORT, HIGH, LOW, THIN, WIDE

MATHEMATICAL GAMES FOR ONE OR TWO

ODDS AND EVENS

PROBABILITY

RIGHT ANGLES: Paper-Folding Geometry

RUBBER BANDS, BASEBALLS AND DOUGHNUTS:
A Book About Topology

STRAIGHT LINES, PARALLEL LINES,
PERPENDICULAR LINES

WEIGHING & BALANCING

WHAT IS SYMMETRY?

Edited by Dorothy Bloomfield, Mathematics Specialist, Bank Street College of Education

ANGLES ARE EASY AS PIE

AREA

AVERAGES

BASE FIVE

BINARY NUMBERS

BUILDING TABLES ON TABLES:
A Book About Multiplication

EXPLORING TRIANGLES:
Paper-Folding Geometry

A GAME OF FUNCTIONS

THE GREATEST GUESSING GAME:
A Book About Dividing

HOW DID NUMBERS BEGIN?

HOW LITTLE AND HOW MUCH:
A Book About Scales

LESS THAN NOTHING IS REALLY SOMETHING

MAPS, TRACKS, AND THE BRIDGES OF KÖNIGSBERG:
A Book About Networks

MEASURE WITH METRIC

NUMBER IDEAS THROUGH PICTURES

ROMAN NUMERALS

SHADOW GEOMETRY

666 JELLYBEANS! ALL THAT?
An Introduction to Algebra

SOLOMON GRUNDY, BORN ON ONEDAY:
A Finite Arithmetic Puzzle

SPIRALS

STATISTICS

3D, 2D, 1D

VENN DIAGRAMS

YES-NO; STOP-GO:
Some Patterns in Logic

ZERO IS NOT NOTHING

Library of Congress Cataloging in Publication Data. Sitomer, Mindel. Zero is not nothing. (A young math book) Summary: Discusses the importance of zero in the decimal system and its many uses. 1. Zero (The number)—Juvenile literature. [1. Zero (The number)] I. Sitomer, Harry, joint author. II. Cuffari, Richard. III. Title. QA141.3.S57 1978   512.72   77-11562
ISBN 0-690-03829-1 lib. bdg.

1 2 3 4 5 6 7 8 9 10

Zero Is
Not Nothing

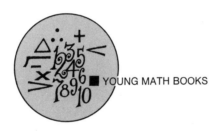

YOUNG MATH BOOKS

Here is a riddle.

It came out of nothing, yet it is something.
When you add it to something, it changes
nothing.

What is it?

Have you ever asked for another cookie and
been told there were no more?
When you spend your last pennies, you have
none left.

The Blue Team beat the Red Team three to nothing.

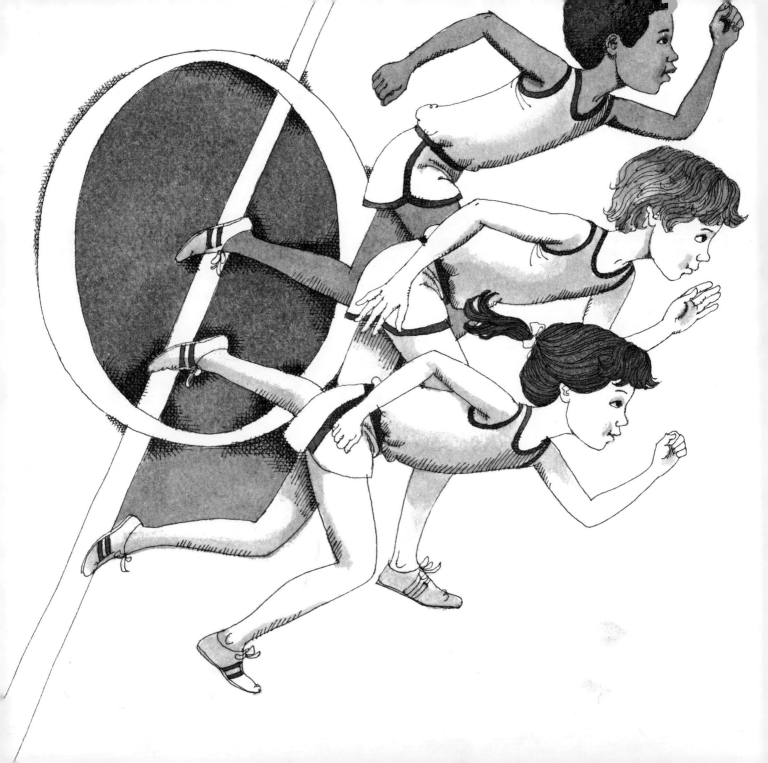

In mathematics there is a symbol which can show there are no more cookies, no pennies, or no points. That symbol is 0. It is called ZERO.

Zero has many uses, all of them important.

Do you know that zero can be a starting place?

Before a race, runners are told "Get on your mark!" The race starts at this mark, and this is sometimes called the zero point of the race.

Zero is the starting point of any race.

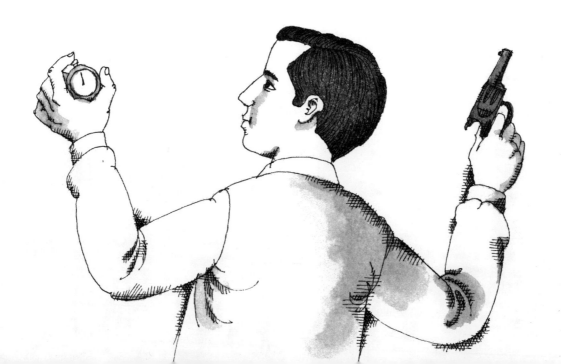

On some scales, a dial points to numbers to show weight. Before you step on the scale, there is no weight on it, and the dial is at zero. After you step on it, it will point to your weight.

Zero is the starting point of any measure of weight.

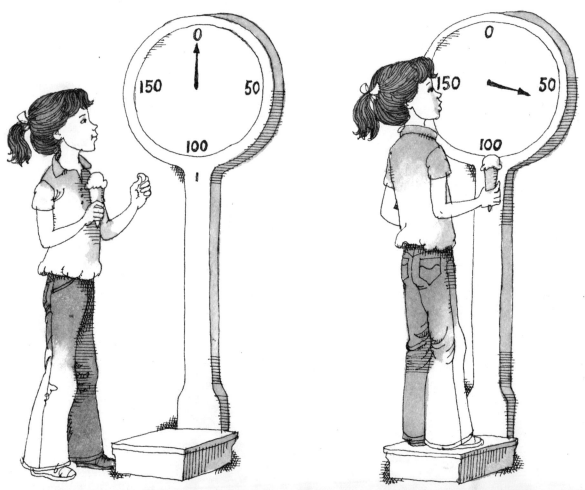

Count the dots on this line.

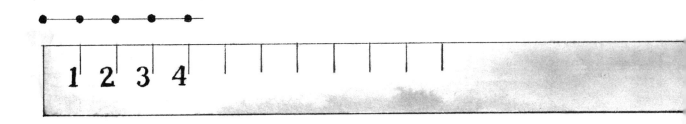

What number did you start with? Of course it was 1.

Now measure the same line with a ruler. Would you place the 1 of the ruler on the first dot? No, the edge of the ruler should be there. There are five dots but only four centimeters. When you count how many centimeters, you say "1" for the first dot after the zero dot. Zero is at the edge of the ruler, just as the dial of a scale with nothing on it is at zero. (Most rulers do not show 0 at the edge because it is taken for granted.)

Zero is the start of any measurement.

Zero can be a separation point.

In the game of Giant Steps or May I?, you may
be told to take 3 steps forward, or 2 steps
backward. Before you have moved one way or the
other, you have taken no steps. You are at zero.

When a rocket is being sent into space, the countdown ends . . . 5 4 3 2 1 Blast Off. As the flight begins, the count is continued 1 2 3 4 5 . . . .

Blast Off is the zero point separating the time before the rocket takes off from the time after the rocket takes off.

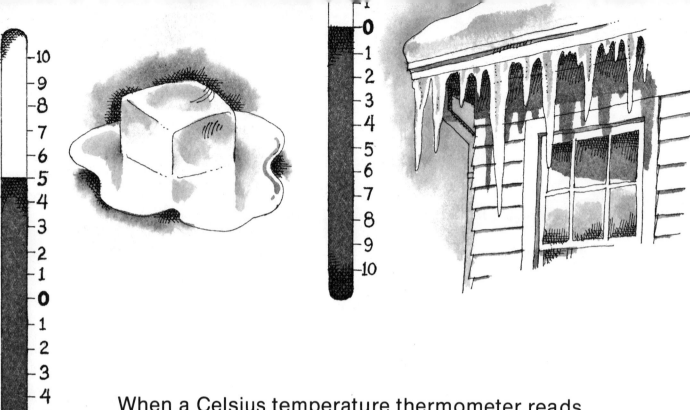

When a Celsius temperature thermometer reads 5° the weather is quite cool. It is colder when it reads 0°. And it is still colder when it reads 5° below 0°. It does not mean there is no temperature at 0°. Water freezes at 0° Celsius. It will melt above 0° and stay frozen below 0°.

On a Celsius thermometer, zero is the separation point between freezing and melting of water.

Zero can be a separation point.

11

Zero can also be a "break-even" point.

If you start a game with 10 marbles and end with 12, you have won 2 marbles. If you end with 8, you have lost 2. If you end with 10, you are even. You have neither won nor lost any.

A storekeeper hopes to make a profit on his sales. Sometimes he has to take a loss. If he "breaks even" he has made no profit, but neither has he lost any money.

Zero can be a "break-even" point.

Here is another very important use for zero.
We need zero for the way we write our numerals.
A dime and three pennies are worth thirteen
cents, which you would write 13¢. The 3 stands for
the three pennies, and the 1 stands for the one
dime. The place of the 3 and the place of the 1 are

important. Thirty-one cents (31¢) is very different from thirteen cents (13¢), even though they use the same symbols, 1 and 3.

When we write any numeral like 13, the symbol at the right means how many pennies or ones. The symbol at the left means how many dimes, or tens.

In the numeral 22, the 2 at the right means two ones. The 2 at the left means two tens. If you had a numeral with three places like 222, the last 2 at the left would mean two hundreds.

Even though each of the symbols in 222 is the same, the value of each 2 is not the same. There are 2 hundreds, 2 tens, and 2 ones. Each 2 in 222 gets its value from its place in the numeral.

That is why we call our system of writing numerals a PLACE VALUE SYSTEM.

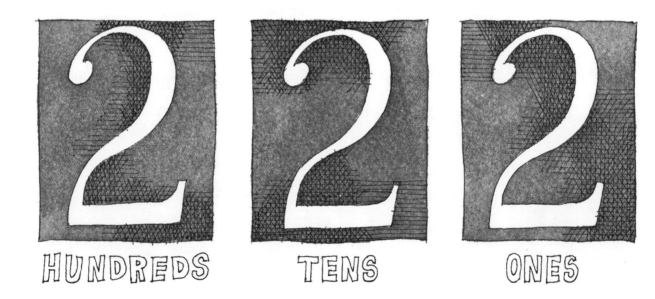

HUNDREDS   TENS   ONES

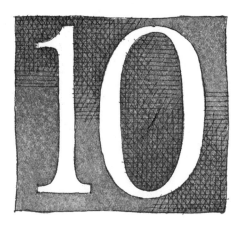

If you had only a dime, you would still write 1 in the tens place to show that 1 dime is worth ten cents. You have no pennies and show it by writing 0 in the ones place. Without 0, when you write 1, it means one penny instead of one dime.

A single numeral by itself means pennies or ones.

The next time your family does a large grocery shopping, look at the cash receipt. You will see the cost of each item listed one below the other in columns. For each price, the pennies are at the right, the dimes are next to the pennies, and the dollars are at the left, next to the dimes. When the ones, tens, and hundreds are listed in columns this way, it is much easier to read or to add them.

Were there any zeros on your receipt?

Zero holds the place in the ones column when there are no pennies. In the same way, zero holds places in other columns.

On your receipt you will also see there are no more than ten different symbols: 1, 2, 3, 4, 5, 6, 7, 8, 9, 0. With just these ten and our place value system, we can write numerals as large as we like. Notice that 0 is one of the symbols.

1.00
2.20
1.04
.90
.75
2.07
3.81
.65
4.15
.10

total 16.67

How did this symbol for zero find its way into our place value system?

Place value systems took many years to develop and people in different parts of the world found their own ways. Here is one.

Many years ago on a large island named Madagascar, in the Indian Ocean, the people wanted to know exactly how many soldiers they had. They used pebbles and a place value system to find out.

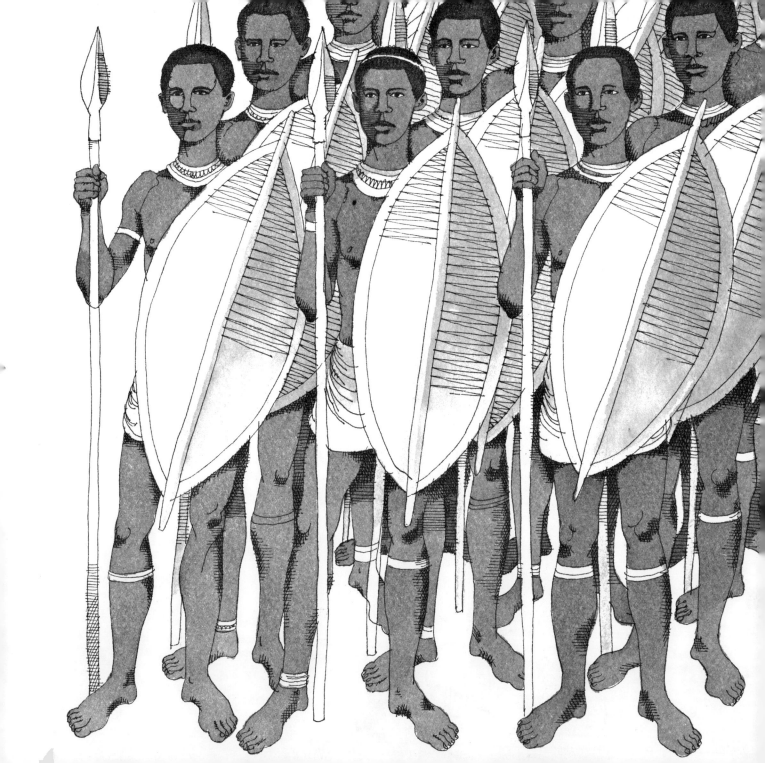

First they drew three circles on the ground using them as we do our places. (You can draw three circles on your paper.)

Hundreds   Tens   Ones

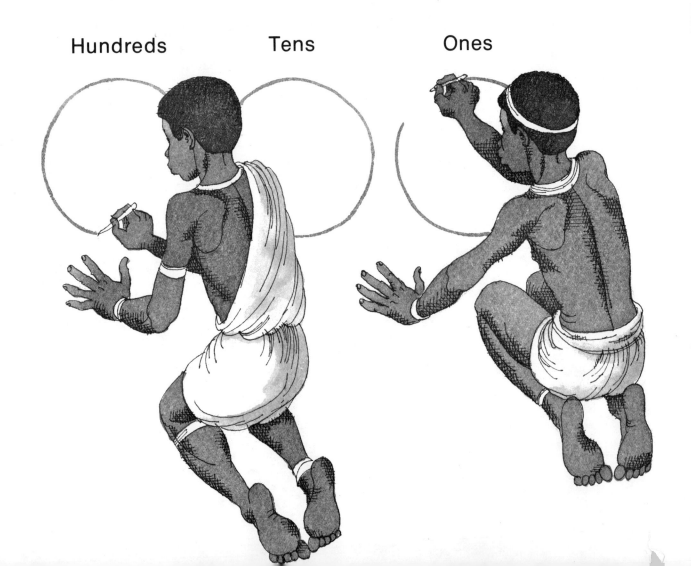

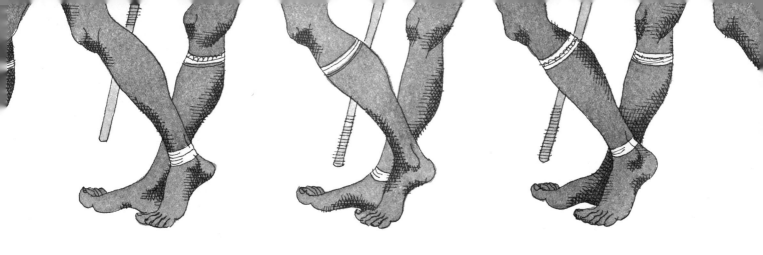

Then the soldiers were lined up in single file and marched slowly past the circles. As the first soldier passed, a single pebble was put in the ones circle. As the next soldier passed, a second pebble was put in the same circle. This went on until the ones circle had nine pebbles.

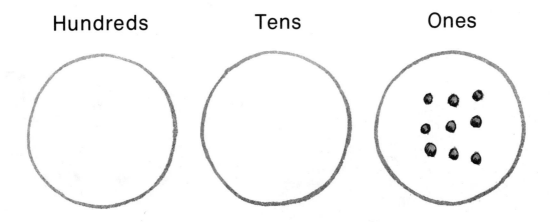

Hundreds   Tens   Ones

When the tenth soldier passed this circle, all nine pebbles were scooped up and just one pebble placed in the tens circle. This was like changing ten pennies into one dime.

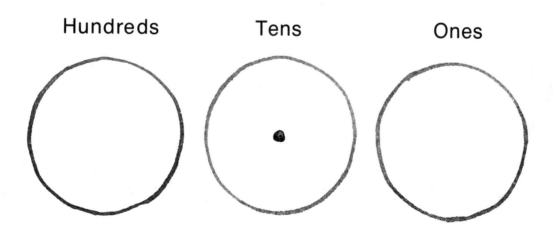

Hundreds	Tens	Ones

Use a paper and pencil and some pebbles or counters to count soldiers along with the story.

As the next nine soldiers passed, one pebble was put in the ones circle for each.

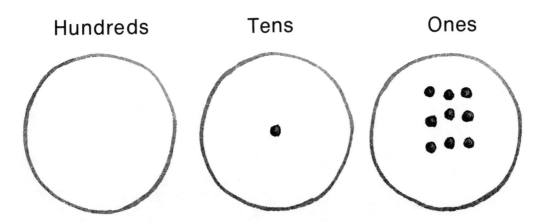

Hundreds	Tens	Ones

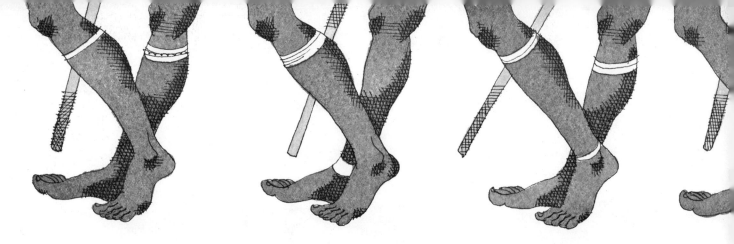

When the next soldier passed, once more the nine pebbles were scooped up and another pebble was put in the tens circle. They never put more than nine pebbles in a circle. As soon as the count was going to be more than nine, they took the pebbles out of it, moved over, and put a pebble in the next circle to the left.

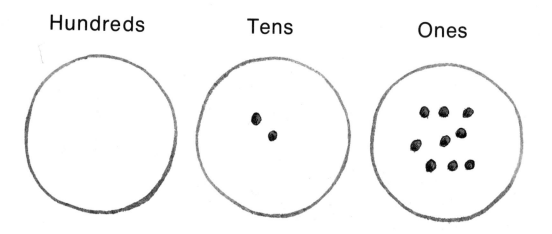

Hundreds   Tens   Ones

The counting continued until the ones circle had nine pebbles and the tens circle also had nine pebbles.

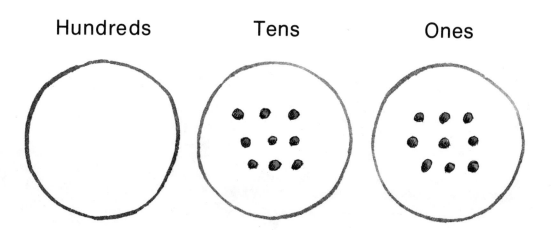

Hundreds   Tens   Ones

When another soldier passed, the nine pebbles of the ones circle were scooped up. But this time, they did not put another pebble in the tens circle. They never put more than nine pebbles in any circle. Instead, the nine pebbles in this circle were also scooped up. One pebble was put in the hundreds circle, just as we change ten dimes into one dollar.

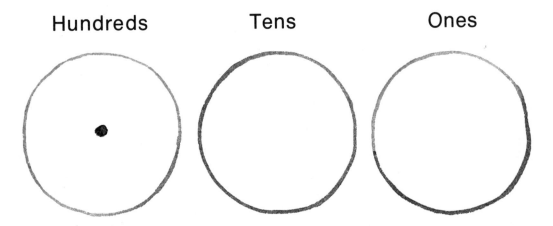

Hundreds   Tens   Ones

When the next soldier passed, the ones circle had one pebble in it again.

Suppose that when the last soldier had passed, the three circles had looked like this:

Hundreds   Tens   Ones

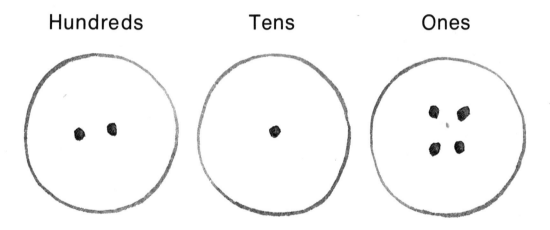

Without many pebbles, they were able to say that there were 2 hundreds, 1 ten, and 4 ones, or a total of 214 men in their army.

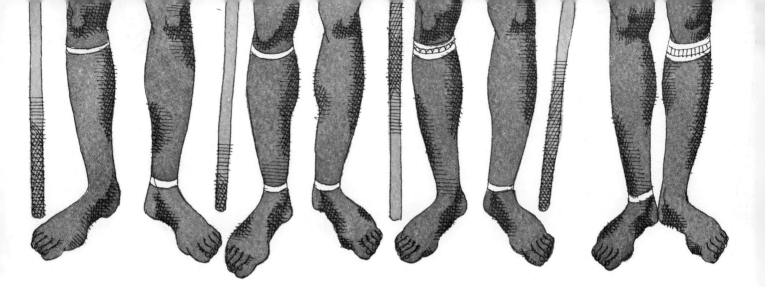

But what if their circles had ended up looking like this?

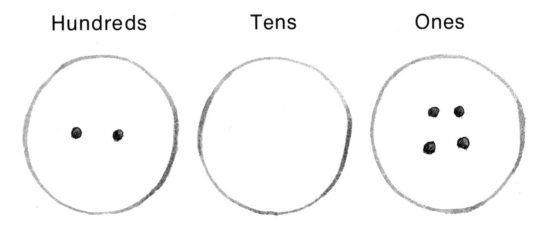

Hundreds   Tens   Ones

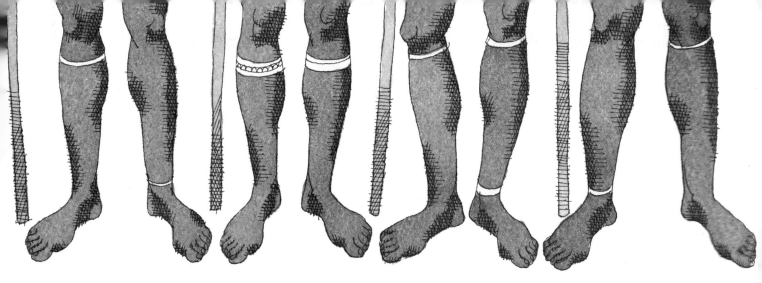

There had to be a symbol to show there were no tens.

You know that a 2 and a 4 could mean 24. Zero in 204 tells us there are no tens. The 2 in 204 means 2 hundreds and the zero holds the place for tens since there aren't any.

In any place value system, whenever there is an empty space in any numeral it is shown by the symbol for zero.

The Hindus in India, about three thousand years ago, were among the earliest people to use a symbol for zero. It was a dot, or a little circle like an **o**. They called it a *sunya,* which meant "empty space."

Some years later, the Arabs learned about this symbol from the Hindus. They found it useful, and took it back to their own countries. They called it a *zifr.* Later, the symbol found its way to Europe.

Still later, it found its way around the world to us.

The Hindu little circle gave us our symbol 0, and the Arabic word zifr changed and became our word *zero*.

These are just some of the ways in which we use zero, and now you know that zero is not nothing.

Do you know the answer to the riddle on page one?

ABOUT THE AUTHORS

ZERO IS NOT NOTHING is the sixth book on which Mr. and Mrs. Sitomer have collaborated. Harry Sitomer, educated in New York City, has taught mathematics in high school and colleges and is an author of textbooks for several experimental mathematics syllabi related to the "new math." He is a coauthor of a textbook on linear algebra. He is also an enthusiastic cellist and gets much enjoyment from his regular sessions with amateur string quartets.

Mindel Sitomer, also educated in New York City, as a biologist, found that their own two children and seven grandchildren had no difficulty in understanding large scientific concepts at an early age. Hence her enjoyment in working with her husband on these books for young readers. She also brailles books for blind children.

The Sitomers make their home in Huntington, New York.

ABOUT THE ILLUSTRATOR

Richard Cuffari's paintings have been exhibited in several New York galleries. A number of his illustrations have appeared in the design shows of the American Institute of Graphic Arts and in the annual exhibits of the Society of Illustrators.

A native of New York, Mr. Cuffari studied at Pratt Institute. He lives in Brooklyn with his children.